*This book is dedicated to my friends Aaron &
Cherie White and Joyce & Callum Rees and all who
give their time to the men and women in the
Downtown Eastside of Vancouver. This is a place
where I've learnt more than any other about
Francis and caring for others as he did.*

Published 2014 by Proost
www.proost.co.uk

Artwork: Jess Freeman

ISBN 978-1-906340-27-8

INTRODUCTION

"For the past 33 years, I have looked in the mirror every morning and asked myself: 'If today were the last day of my life, would I want to do what I am about to do today?' And whenever the answer has been 'No' for too many days in a row, I know I need to change something."
Steve Jobs, Cofounder of Apple [1]

It was one of those moments when the whole world was watching.

Despite the common conception that we live in a world turning it's back on religion, billions of television viewers joined the thousands in St Peter's Square in Rome to watch a small little chimney churn out white smoke rather than the usual black.   This comical and definitely outdated smoke signal has announced Popes for centuries and there was something surreal about the images of people holding iPads and phone cameras to take

---

[1] *Steve Jobs addressing students at Stanford University 12 June 2005*

a picture of the most untechnical system in modern day life.

Earlier that day two seagulls had settled down on the chimney and made this their temporary home. These little birds had in an instant become a TV and internet hit, even opening their own @SisteneSeagull twitter account. Questioned about the unlikely celebrity of the drawn out Conclave a Vatican representative suggested the bird might be the Holy Spirit. A few polite giggles ensued but he might have had the last laugh as hours later the 2013 Conclave produced an unexpected Spirit-inspired Pope, cheered on by a little man from Assisi who loved to care for birds. Something remarkable was happening.

The white smoke billowing from the chimney was greeted by gasps and cheers. Not long after Vatican soldiers in ornate uniforms began to appear and the stage was set for the announcement. Although smoke confirmed that an election had taken place no one knew who.

As I watched on TV a variety of commentators lined up to discuss the front runners. These were the likely appointments, especially as the decision had been relatively quick. As I watched my mind went back to those seagulls. What is it that the Holy Spirit had been doing? I was soon to find out.

Pope in black shoes

Habemus Papam! ("We Have a Pope!") is the gleeful declaration by the Vatican official on the balcony of the Vatican. Next would come the chosen name. I stopped for a moment, trying to make out the Latin. Did he say Francis? There had never been a Pope Francis. Benedict, Leo or Pius maybe. What about another John-Paul? But Francis? 'Francesco' had been the Latin word. In amongst all of this no-one actually knew who would be appearing still. The TV commentator seemed a little stunned. Francis I. Although the expert seemed to be stumbling over the name I was off my seat .... "It's Francis of Assisi!! That's who he's named after!!" The moment may have got the better of me but I didn't care.

Then the new Pope arrived. Not a cardinal from Milan or an influential figure from Asia or Africa. Instead an old smiley man emerged called Jorge Mario Berguglio, a Jesuit from Argentina, who until then had been Cardinal of Buenos Aires. Now he was to be known as Pope Francis I.

As I write these pages, Pope Francis has just passed his 100th day in office. He is enacting a quiet revolution. By wearing simple black shoes, by shunning pomp and circumstance or by washing the feet of the poor and needy, this Pope is intent on change. Here is a man seemingly orthodox in theology yet providing revolutionary love and acceptance to those who felt on the outskirts of the world.

As I listened to his simple short initial address to the faithful in Rome I shed a few tears. To someone who had been seeking to study and understand the life of St Francis of Assisi for several years this seemed like an overwhelmingly significant moment.

"I would like to see a church that is poor and for the poor"[2] he said the following day at his first address in front of the world's press. This man from Argentina who was now the most influential Catholic in the world had decided to elevate the broken, poor and excluded rather than elevate his own position. Instead of chauffeur driven cars and an expensive apartment he would live simply still and not forget the poor.

As I reflected on what most news agencies were calling a surprise and landmark appointment I remembered what I had read about Francis of Assisi's first trip to Rome to see a Pope in the Old St. Peter's Basilica which once stood on the site of the many of the halls and buildings Pope Francis had encountered on that March day. This little man had indeed changed the Church and was still changing it today.

---

[2] Lizzy Davies report in the Guardian Newspaper UK 16 March 2013

This little book

This little book of Lent reflections is inspired by this little man who's changed and affected my life. About fifteen years ago I first made contact with something people 'new monasticism' through a 24-7 Prayer room in my home town of Reading. It was a voyage of discovery that has changed my life in some many ways. But one of the things I'm most grateful for is that I'm become more aware of this little saint from Assisi.

It is not simply the 3 million or so pilgrims which visit Francis' tomb in Assisi or the three orders with over 1 million members that makes Francis significant in 2014. Leonardo Boff argues that "our present day culture finds in Francis a great deal of that for which we hunger and thirst.[3]"

It's my experience that today Francis can be a mirror for us as we seek to pioneer new forms of church and mission in our world today.

---

[3] Leonardo Boff 'Francis' New York: Orbis Books 2006 pg. x

"A culture needs historical personalities who serve as mirrors in which that culture may see itself and be convinced of the values that give meaning to being"[4]

I'd like to suggest four mirror images which Francis can provide us as we begin this journey together. Looking into a mirror like this can be incredibly challenging. Peter rightly pointed out that this period of self-reflection began with the church (1 Peter 4:7-10).

Francis is the mirror image of a pioneer minister. He got something started, from scratch and appropriate to his context. Francis has things to teach us about hearing from God, establishing a vision and a reality and of how to relate to the church and the culture around him. I'd like to learn to pioneer like Francis.

Francis is the mirror-image poet leader. He embraced creation and creativity, he loved life and knew how to celebrate. He painted pictures with sermons, and created waves with words. He was a

---

[4] Boff 'Francis' pg. 16

troubadour leader. I'd like to embrace the poetry of faith like Francis.

Francis is the mirror-image pilgrim wanderer. He journeyed, he walked the road and invited others to join him. As we explore the journey of life, I'd like to be a pilgrim like Francis.

Francis is the mirror-image of prophetic mission. He had a message from God for the Church and for society which was ahead of his time. Our Church is crying out for prophetic voices today; I'd like to look for a prophet like Francis.

Finally Francis looked in the mirror to observe the life and words of Christ. He was foremost a disciple. As we embark further into the life of Francis and ask questions of our Church and of faith in the 21st Century it will be both the mirror image of Francis and also this seeking the life of Christ which will be anchors. It's again time for the Church to change as a new cultural epoch begins.

I hope over the next forty days you get the chance to look into this mirror which has made such an impact on my own journey. Jesus would you challenge us and change us as we look together at your servant Francis?

HOW TO USE THIS BOOK

This book comprises of a series of Lent reflections. You can use these at any other time of year too, but Lent feels like the most appropriate place for them. Here's three things which might help you on this journey:

- The book splits into five sections. Each section has eight reflections on a simple theme.

- Each section has an illustration and a story to begin it. The stories are loosely based on historical information on Francis but also allow for some poetic license. There are many historical books about Francis but this book seeks to emphasis a sense of reflection and so story feels more appropriate.

- Each day's reflection has a thought, an activity and prayer. They can be read quickly or reflected on over time. Whatever fits your life and time.

Enjoy.

PART ONE:

MEETING FRANCIS

"Francis created a popular expression of the Church: the mystery of the Church becomes concrete in the small fraternity of brothers in contact with the people and with the poorest of the people of God"
Leonard Boff, Theologian

Story: San Damiano

'Did I hear a voice?'

Francis must have jolted with shock as he knelt before the cross in the church known as San Damiano. But then it came again ...

"Francis, don't you see that my house has collapsed? Go and repair it for me."

The year 1206 had marked some new seasons in the life of Francis. His military career was over after being captured, and imprisoned during the Civil War between the Umbria and Perugia. His year in prison and subsequent severe tuberculosis had led an emaciated Francis to return home. He still dreamed of being a knight but instead he had been led on a new path, through a growing sense of God speaking and a dream to seek a new master. Francis biographer Adrian House suggests that Francis now sought the "noblest, richest and most beautiful bride"[5] in his faith in Christ but he had no idea how to live out this faith and what he should do. Francis waited.

This growing sense of call had found a friend in Bishop Guido of Assisi. The Bishop had heard of Francis' reckless generosity giving large amounts of money and bread to the poor and his first engagements with the leper colony outside Assisi. Now Guido sought to guide him and give him counsel, since God was at work in him.

As Francis waited he took Bishop Guido's advice to seek God wherever he could find him through wandering and pilgrimage. Francis took time to walk the paths and roads of Assisi and it's surrounding area. He spent time praying in caves. He spent time walking and praying. Maybe it was here that his growing sense of the created world around him began to dawn. It was here too that he found the voice of God in the most unlikely place.

---

[5] Adrian House 'Francis of Assisi' London: Pimlico 2001 pg. 51

That day in 1206 he came across the decaying church of San Damiano, less than a mile below Assisi. At first look the building might have been mistaken for being empty or unused. It's roof was fallen in, windows broken, holes in the walls remaining in disrepair. Francis peered in and saw a priest busying himself with tasks around the building. Realising that the church was indeed still open he walked in, hoping he might find some seclusion to pray.

In amongst the rubble with birds flying in through holes he sensed peace and he walked to the front near the altar and knelt to pray. This had become a familiar position to Francis. Bishop Guido had guided him into a life of study and prayer and he was beginning to understand the weight of discipleship and the commitment to pray which lay at it's heart.

As he prayed maybe his mind took some time to settle. Thoughts of his father who did not yet know of his newfound faith or his generosity to the poor of the neighbourhood might have tried to sneak into his thoughts. What would his father do if he found out? Concern for his mother who did know of his actions and had been covering for him. Yearnings to discover what this pilgrimage was all about and what God intended for him. Slight pangs of hunger interrupted these thoughts as it had been a while since he had been able to eat.

Then as he settled himself he focused on the icon of Christ on the cross which hung above the altar. Francis had been trained to understand the practice of meditating before icons. He should look for the detail the artist had included and allow it speak to him. He peered intently at the image of Christ and then he was stunned by what he thought was a voice.

'Francis, don't you see that my house has collapsed? Go and repair it for me.'

Francis looked around briefly. Taken aback by the experience. He could not see the Priest and no one else seemed to be in the building. He looked again at the icon and felt the same voice speaking to him again. He realised this was the voice of God.

Francis took little time to consider or interpret the words as they seemed clear to him. He got up, and sought out the priest of the church and giving him money for oil for the lamp on the altar, asking that the lamp not go out. It was almost like Francis needed to mark the moment like Jacob or Abraham in those early stories in Genesis. That lamp was his Bethel altar.

The next day Francis returned with supplies to re-roof the building. The priest, knowing Francis and his family knew this was being funded by money from Francis' father Pietro's income. He stood in Francis' way and said no, fearing the backlash that might come his way. Not for the last time in his life Francis was persistent, offering to do the work with his bare hands.

The rebuilding of the church at San Damiano became Francis' passion for the next two years.

Day 1

Thought

About 800 years ago Francis of Assisi felt a call from God to rebuild the church. At first he did this with bricks and mortar but over time he realised his call was for the metaphorical rebuilding of the Church itself. In 2014 we live in a time where the Church across the world is being shaken. What would this sort of rebuilding look like today? What's our part?

Activity

Go for a walk around your village, town or city. Go and find church buildings of different denominations and stand outside them for a while. Pray silent prayers for the rebuilding and renewing of the church.

Prayer

God of the Church. We're sorry we've made your body about bricks and mortar. Rebuild the church and start with our hearts. Amen.

Day 2

Thought

Francis took his call seriously, formed an order of Franciscans and eventually took his fellow brothers and his rule of life to Pope Innocent for his approval. He wanted to change the church but wanted to work with it too. The Pope was amazed by Francis and approved what they were doing.

Activity

Collect a week's newspapers. Look for stories about the church. Build up a reflection of how ourculture views the Church. Look for repeated words or phrases. Turn the reflections into a blog post or article. Ask for comment and opinions. Pray into your conclusions and ask others to join you.

Prayer

Take five minutes of silence and meditate on today's church and your place in it. Ask God to speak to you about your place in it and your place to challenge it and to re-imagine it.

Day 3

Thought

Writer and historian Marina Warner suggests that "the Franciscan spirit continues to be considered by agnostics and atheists as well as believers as the most genuine expression of Christ's teaching ever approved by the Vatican.[6]" Francis seems to be able to stand in a unique position in a post-church world as someone deeply respected for his beliefs and actions. What do you think it means to be a genuine and authentic Christian? How can we live in this way?

Activity

Take some salt and place it in the palm of your hand. Salt is a natural preserver and purifier. Take a pinch of salt between your fingers and feel it's texture. Consider your own walk with God and also for the salt of the Spirit to be at work in you.

Prayer

Holy Spirit speak to my heart. Help me to live the sort of life which speaks of Christ to others. Amen

---

[6] Boff Francis pg. 41

Day 4

Thought

Francis' spirituality was in tune with the world he lived in and the earth he walked in. Boff wrote "through his deep humanity Francis of Assisi has become an archetype of the human ideal: open to God, universal brother, and caretaker of nature and of mother Earth. He belongs not only to Christianity but to all mankind.[7]"

Activity

As you go about your day today find a moment to stop and to stand on the earth/ground. This is the place God has put you in. This is the earth that is His and a gift to you. Take in your surroundings today with thankfulness.

Prayer

The earth is the Lord's and everything in it. Psalm 24:1. Repeat this verse over and over and allow it to sink in. Use this as a prayer.

---

[7] Boff Francis pg. x

Day 5

Thought

One the the incredible dynamics of early Franciscans was their complete rejection of property and wealth. The brothers and sisters committed to poverty as a way of life, begging when they needed to as a way of sharing solidarity with the poor. Francis only asked for what he really needed and that wasn't much.

Activity

Bishop Graham Cray suggests that consumerism is a strong force in our culture and "makes disciples more effectively than the Church.[8]" Go for a walk round the shops of your town and reflect on this. What is God saying?

Prayer

Jesus Christ, Light of the World, bring light into the world around me. Thank you that you are all that we need. Help us to believe that too. Amen

---

[8] Graham Cray "New Monasticism as a Fresh Expression of Church" Canterbury Press 2010 pg.3

Day 6

Thought

At San Damiano Francis encountered the voice of God for the first time. This type of story can make us feel jealous or doubtful. Why doesn't God speak clearly to me? Yet this incident took place years after Francis had begun loving and serving the poorest in his town. Francis met Jesus first in the needs of people and the voice at San Damiano took years not minutes to come.

Activity

The Bible encourages us time and again to wait on the Lord. Go to somewhere in your town where people wait. Join a queue. Wait at a bus stop. Whilst you wait pray to God about what you'd like him to speak to you about.

Prayer

Voice of the living God, speak into my life. Speak to my soul. Speak to my dreams and hopes. Speak to my fears. Speak Lord, and we will try to listen. Amen

Day 7

Thought

A look at the life of Francis would suggest he was into everything. He did social justice. He organised a movement. He wanted to change the church. He preached. He prayed. But to Francis the gospel message he shared was all about replicating the life of Jesus. He read the gospels and wanted to live them out.

Activity

Find a full length mirror and pray as you look into it. What does God want to show you about your life? How can you reflect Jesus in how you live?

Prayer

Write yourself a prayer about how you might be more Christ-like. Seal it in an envelope, address it and give it to a friend. Ask them to post it to you in 3 months.

Day 8

Thought

Francis spent years rebuilding the church at San Damiano. He learnt more about discipleship and service as he served others - the local priest, the church community, the local area. Sometimes we ponder about what our life is when there is a task we can get going on. Sometimes it's right to get on and take action.

Activity

Design and make a simple mosaic design. I have suggested mosaic for a reason as it takes time (check out a design on the internet if you've never done this before). Use whatever materials you can find. Choose a design that says something about your soul and your faith. As you lay each tile, consider what makes up your spirituality and what feeds your soul. As each tile goes down either thank God or ask him for help, depending on where you feel. When you finish put the mosaic somewhere where you pray as a reminder of the San Damiano soul-work going on in your life.

Prayer

Father God, as I reflect more on the life of Francis help me to understand how you're speaking to me and how I might live. Work on my soul and help me to soften my heart to serve others and to be open to God. Amen

PART TWO:

MEETING THE POOR

"Poverty is the worst form of violence."

Mahatma Gandhi

Story: Encounter

Francis was doing all he could to stop himself vomiting.

He had met lepers before and if he was honest had tried to stay as far away as possible. His first encounter as a child had revolted and scared him. Italian culture in those days made sure that lepers were isolated and removed from normal life. Francis had never questioned this position, always being quite glad of the sound of the clapper that any leper had to shake to make people aware of their presence. He was quite happy to avoid them.

However, as Francis was now beginning the reorientation of his life he felt challenged to change his position. Francis stood in front of this man on the road outside Assisi. He did not know his name, his story or anything about him. What he knew all about at that moment was the smell of putrefying flesh. He was not sure whether it was the sight that afflicted his eyes or the horrible stench which assaulted his nose but Francis feared lepers. Now a fresh commitment and faith compelled him to act differently.

He had been building up to this moment for weeks. He knew this was the greatest challenge God had put before him so far. Francis knew Jesus had loved those who others considered unlovable. He knew he was called to do the same and instantly knew the mostly unlovable in his community were those who lived in the Lazar House two miles outside the city.

Leprosy is a disease which has affected humanity for over 4,000 years. Today it's anticipated 2-3 million people are disabled because of the disease, but the World Health Organisation anticipates 15 million have been cured over the past 20 years.[9]

In Francis' time leprosy was a death sentence. It was a common and horrible disease with skin swelling, breaking up or changing colour. Those suffering might have crippled limbs and could lose hair, fingers or even noses. Town's responded by

---

[9] Adrian House 'Francis of Assisi' London: Pimlico 2001 pg. 85

throwing out those who suffered. Infection was the predominant fear but there was plenty of prejudice mixed in too. Lazar houses sprung up well outside city limits well away from the population and busy trade and travel routes.

Adding to their disgrace, lepers would be forced to wear a distinctive grey cloak and have a wooden clapper or rattle to shake as they walked which made sure anyone could get out of the way if they were walking the same road. A leper could not enter the town or city, not attend any public gatherings and were even restricted in the way they could beg. As a leper entered a Lazar House they would be met by a priest who would declare them dead to the world. Leprosy left no room for remaining dignity.

Standing opposite of Francis at that moment stood a man who looked broken on the inside as well as broken and damaged physically. Somewhere deep within him, suppressing all the horror he felt, Francis found grace, courage and most of all compassion. Francis stepped down from his horse, gave the man a coin and then gently kissed his head. Deeply moved, the leper kissed him in return.

At this point in the story a considerable amount of myth and legend exists. It appears that as Francis remounted his horse he looked around and could no longer see the man. Biographers suggest at that minute Francis realised he had kissed the face of Christ is the guise of a leper.[10]

Whether this was a metaphorical or actual meeting what is clear is that Jesus did indeed meet Francis at that moment and changed his heart. Days later, Francis returned to the Lazar House with a large amount of money and distributed it amongst them, kissing each in turn. As he continued to care, he and the fellow friars who were to join him spent considerable time in the leper communities that were around them, nursing wherever they could. One particularly beautiful story tells of Francis washing a man who was leprous in scented water,

---

[10] John V Kruse 'Lent and Easter Wisdom from St Francis and St Clare of Assisi' Missouri: Ligouri 2008

praying for him as he was washed. Although the man died later it was said he departed in great peace. This act of kindness was something that would have been unpalatable to the younger Francis. He had changed.

Francis later shared that it was here God inspired him to the way of life he would embark on and that would be so inspirational to others (the voice in the chapel at San Damiano came after years of caring for the poor). In his Testament, Francis writes "what had previously nauseated me became the source of spiritual and physical consolation for me."[11]   It seems each time Francis met a leper from that moment he met Christ in their pain and suffering, he met Christ in their humanity.

---

[11] Quote from Francis 'Testament' quoted in Shaine Claibourne 'The Irresistible Revolution' Michigan: Zondervan pg. 37

Day 9

Thought

The most radical thing about Francis was not his care for lepers - many others in the established church did this. What set him apart though was that he cared from amongst people. He spent time living with those suffering with leprosy. He was present, risking much to love people.

Activity

Many compare Francis' approach to care to the incarnation - Jesus becoming present amongst us. Is there an issue or concern that is important to you? How could you be present? Maybe this will be a visit, a phone call or maybe about you committing time and energy to a cause. Reflect and then act.

Prayer

Present God, be with me day by day.
Loving God, may your presence comfort those who are poor, broken or excluded this day.
Amen

Day 10

Thought

What did the incarnation mean to St. Francis? Leonardo Boff suggests "the incarnation is, for Francis, a mystery of divine sympathy and empathy.[12]" Somehow the incarnation encourages us towards not just caring but connecting and sharing somehow with the poor or excluded.

Activity

Take a piece of paper and divide it in two. Write Sympathy at the top of one side and Empathy on the other. Then on each side write words or ideas which connect with these words. Allow this exercise to ask you questions of how you care for others and how you might do so in the future.

Prayer

Jesus Christ, Son of God. You were born as a human, lived a human life and died a human death. This was the way you loved us. Show us how to love in a similar way and teach us more about your incarnation. Amen

---

[12] Boff 'Francis' pg. 23

Day 11

Thought

A phrase common to many Franciscan texts is *"sequi vestigial et paupertatem eius"* which literally means 'to follow in his footsteps and poverty.' As the community developed around him, Francis' rule of life put this principle at the core of their identity. Francis saw that Jesus associated himself with the poorest in his world.

Activity

Go for a walk somewhere where you can make footprints - a beach, a muddy field. If you can't do that roll out some paper and walk on it using paint or something else. Look back at your steps and ask what it means to walk in the steps of Jesus in your life.

Prayer

Teach me Lord to walk in your footprints in this day and each day coming. Take me on your journeys. Help me to walk like you walked. Amen

Day 12

Thought

Francis believed that "God made himself our brother in poverty and humility."[13] In his naturally poetic style he would speak of Holy Lady Poverty and esteem the lowest in the society in which he lived: those who 'mourn', the 'meek' or those who were 'poor in spirit.' To Francis they were highly valued and in them he found Jesus.

Activity

Do some research into your local community? Who are the outcasts in your society? Who have been sent to the outskirts of your town and city like the leper's of Francis time? Maybe this is refugees seeking asylum or a community that seeks to live differently, maybe homelessness or an illness or condition? Take time to research the history of this exclusion and the issues involved. If you can go and visit these people. How can you and those around you love people who are excluded? How can you champion their cause or seek a different way of living?

---

[13] Boff 'Francis' pg. 23

Prayer

Most High God who loves and cares for those in poverty - would you give esteem and honour to the poorest today. Maybe we might not see this but we ask you might grant grace and encouragement to those whose lives are very tough. Amen

Day 13

Thought

Francis loved other human beings most of all because they were other human beings. They were unique and given great dignity by the fact they are each made in the image of God. Francis was compelled by the task of loving others often acting in secret.

Activity

Go for a walk in your High Street. Take two trips up and down it. On your first walk look at all the advertisements in windows. Stop at the end and ask what they say about views of human beings? Then take a second walk and observe people. Spend some time praying and thanking God that we are all unique and made in His image.

Prayer

Jesus you are the truest Image of God. Help us to mirror something of your spirit in our humanity and help us to honour all those around us, made in the same way. Amen

Day 14

Thought

Francis' approach was not simply about being kind. It is here also where we find Jesus himself and meet with Him in new ways. Just as Francis kissed the leper and then realised he may well have kissed the face of Jesus, we also find our Saviour in the unlikely lives of ordinary people struggling to survive.

Activity

Scan through a newspaper. magazine or internet news stories and look for images of those involved in the stories. Look into their faces and ask God to speak to you.

Prayer

Loving God. Help me to love other people well today and as I do so help me to be expectant that you might show yourself in their lives. Amen

Day 15

Thought

Theologians Bevans & Schroeder comment that Francis lived and preached a different view of Christ in the way he loved the unloved in his world. This was "Christ of the poor and in the poor. Christ in a leper speaking to Francis or from the crucifix in the dilapidated chapel of San Damiano."[14]

Activity

Find three religious images of Jesus to ponder. What is our view of Jesus. What does Francis' view of Jesus say to these images or challenge them?

Prayer

Pray silently in front of an icon or image of Christ. Speak to us God.

Amen

---

[14] Steven Bevans/Roger Schroeder "Constants in Context: A Theology of Mission for Today" New York: Orbis 2004 pg. 166

Day 16

Thought

Francis did not disconnect mission and social justice. He did not consider anyone more important than the Holy Lady Poverty. He made sure he never forgot the poor and made sure others around him also did not forget. "The greatness of Saint Francis consisted in seeing the poor with the eyes of the poor, allowing him, hungry and thirsty, to discover the values of the poor."[15]

Activity

Take two flasks or jugs and fill one with water and leave one empty. Slowly over a time pour the water out of one and into the other. Repeat this many time as meditation. What does it mean that Jesus was poured out for us (Luke 22:20)? Take some time to reflect on your own life and what these ideas of self-emptying mean to you.

Prayer

Christ poured out for us be our inspiration. Amen

---

[15] Boff 'Francis' pg. 46

MEETING PEOPLE ON THE WAY ..

"Never doubt that a small group of thoughtful,
committed citizens can change the world; indeed,
it's the only thing that ever has"
Margaret Mead: American Cultural Anthropologist

STORY: CROSSING LINES

Francis made many journeys and encountered many people along the way. This story shares just one of those journeys.

As Francis walked through the encampments of the Crusaders his mind drifted briefly back to those early years in his life when his only desire was to be a knight. In his early twenties this sort of campaign would have appealed, now it appalled.

His traveling companion Brother Illuminato walked quietly beside him. This was to be a serious journey. It was 1219 and they were standing in the middle of the Western armies in the campaign of the 5th Crusade - the camp was led by Jean de Brienne, commander of the Crusading army. Their destination was Damieta in Egypt and to cross enemy lines to visit the Sultan Al-Malik al-Kamil. They had no idea how they would be received or whether they would even reach their destination alive.

The Crusades had been in the background of politics and religion throughout Francis' life, a little like the war on terror has so punctuated the last few generations today. The Crusades had begun in 1095 with the 1st Crusade to liberate Jerusalem from invading armies from a coalition of Muslim nations. Whilst that Crusade had been successful (in terms of it's objective) others hadn't been and as these bloody wars developed they had become as much about ensuring the power of Rome as they had any sense of religious virtue (indeed they had never been about that). In the 4th Crusade, troops loyal to the Pope went and attacked Constantinople, the centre of the Eastern Christian Church for good measure. Ethics, values and goals had well and truly got subsumed into primal urges of violence and control.

Francis and Illuminato were traveling to see the Sultan and to attempt to stop the war. They had no tools but love and respect, and although they were probably intent on trying to convert the Sultan, they went with a tolerance and appreciation of fellow human beings that was ultimately to be their greatest weapon. This is Francis, fighting revolutions of love and peace rather than violence again.

After several hours of travelling they reached the camp of the Sultan's army. Initially they were arrested and understandably the Sultan's troops were cautious of these two unarmed European men arriving in their stronghold. Some reports suggest that the brothers were beaten at first but clearly after discovering they were holy men they were received by the Sultan and indeed received warmly. He offered them hospitality and kindness which Francis and Illuminato received with thanks and with great respect.

Over several days the men talked and reasoned together. The Sultan was an intelligent man, well read and he was deeply sick of war. He admired Francis and questioned him at great length. Francis too began to be drawn to the Sultan and observed with an incredible attitude of learning the practices and ways of the Islamic faith. Particularly striking to him was the call to prayer and it's regularity. It made such an impression that on his return Francis instigated something similar.

In all they spent two days together before some of the Sultan's men escorted Francis and Illuminato back behind the European lines. The war did not end until 1221 and there is no discernible change in the faith or understanding of the Sultan after their meeting. The implications of this event though, ripple through to today with people of Muslim faith deeply impressed and respectful of the life and work of St. Francis. Francis took nonviolence and peacemaking and threw himself into the chaos of the Crusades. Some of the greatest affects of this incredible journey will remain hidden forever.

Day 17

Thought

In this section we will look at some encounters Francis had. Our story shares about his meetings with the Sultan during the crusades. This was a love of an enemy and the journey of a peacemaker. Francis offered dignity, honour and love to a leader that many despised.

Activity

All of our communities have barriers, whether physical, practical or psychological. Investigate your community and go and stand at a barrier. Ask God to heal wounds and to bring about peace.

Prayer

Prince of Peace, we pray for the barriers in our world both at home and in the far flung places of the earth. We pray for peace where division exists. As we pray help us play our part. Amen

Day 18

Thought

Francis began his spiritual journey alone but soon met other people who asked to join him. He gave them brown tunics like his and they committed to pray, to poverty and to sharing their faith through service and words. Francis worked in community and friendship. There are over a million Franciscans today.

Activity

Take some paper and cut out some images of people. Write names on the cut outs and spend time thanking God for people who walk with you. How might you serve and love them?

Prayer

Thank you God for our friends. We name each before you. Bless and keep our dear friends. Amen

Day 19

Thought

These brothers then went out on journeys of mission all over Italy and into other parts of Europe. They walked everywhere. It is recorded their journeys could be tracked by their blood stained footprints in the snow in the winter months.

Activity

Take out your wallet or purse and empty the contents. Consider what you have. Consider also what you have lost. What is your view of sacrifice?

Prayer

The biblical writers said every good and perfect gift comes from you God. We thank you for what you've given us and we ask that we might hold it lightly and be prepared even to have bloody footprints as we walk. Amen

Day 20

Thought

The 2nd Franciscan Order is a female order known as the Poor Clare's. Clare was the first woman to join Francis and he took great time and effort to empower and include her. At the time this was a massive innovation. Clare's devotion to Christ meant Francis felt compelled to ask his Bishop to help and to create a women's order at first simply for Clare's benefit. However in a few years score's of women joined her.

Activity

In 2013 Marin Alsop became the first woman to conduct the orchestra on the last night of the Prom's concerts in London. She was amazed that in this era of equality there were still 'firsts'. Thank God for the brave people who've pioneered new things or who've been 'firsts'.

Prayer

Find a woman who has inspired you in the Bible or in History. Write a prayer that reflects their journey. Thank God for them.

Day 21

Thought

Within a short time the Poor Clare's were nearly 50 strong, attracting women from all backgrounds and in time developing an incredible legacy of prayerfulness, compassion & deep devotion to God. Their number included royalty and a dozen saints. Over time, thousands of women would be inspired by Clare's bravery to retreat from the abuse and dominance by men in a male dominated Europe to religious communities of their own gender.

Activity

Go and visit your local school or university. Reflect on the current reality that in many nations women are still deprived basic things like education. Pray for God to change this. Go home and research the issue.

Prayer

God who is our mother and our father, give us grace to value all who make our humanity whatever gender, race, background or anything else which may divide us. Amen

Day 22

Thought

The stories of Clare and others showed Francis has no issue with confronting religion or cultural practices if that was what was needed to follow Christ. He empowered Clare to enable her to be who she was and who she was called to be.

Activity

Take a bible or a prayer book and wrap it in red ribbon. Ponder all the cultural and religious red tape we use to stop things happening. Take some scissors and cut through it. Commit to live as Francis did .... doing what it takes to follow.

Prayer

Empowering God, you could have saved the world all by yourself, yet day by day you ask us to join in. You love to empower us. Help us to empower others.

Day 23

Thought

Francis was often amazed by the people he met and who joined him. In his Testament he confesses to his surprise, saying that the Lord had given him brothers yet had not shown him what to do with them. He committed to pray with them and to love them and in time a path emerged.

Activity

Jesus told the disciples "Take nothing for the journey - no staff, no bag, no bread, no money, no extra shirt." (Luke 9:3). Ponder what this approach means. How often do we depend on resources and knowing the thing to do.

Prayer

God I have nothing but myself to offer. Thank you that that is more than enough. Amen

Day 24

Thought

Francis travelled to many places and received hospitality from many people. Each time he arrived at a new place or met new people on the road he would always offer them peace. This simple blessing has become a Franciscan tradition.

Activity

Go and find a peaceful spot. Maybe a quiet river, a park, a church or a place in your house. Consider what you think peace is. How might you offer it? How does God grant it to us?

Prayer

Peace of Christ fill me.

Peace of Christ be a gift that I may give.

Amen

MEETING WITH MOTHER EARTH

"He made the world to be a grassy road Before her wandering feet."
W. B. Yeates, Poet

STORY: WANDERING

Francis began his journey early. He had a days walk ahead of him but also knew that he didn't want to rush. There was too much of the beauty and glory of God between him and his destination to rush in any way. In any case the idea of a destination was a little hazy to Francis, he knew there would be one and was happy to trust that to God.

After rising he spent time in his prayers, went to see and encourage a few of the brothers before he left and then headed out of the gates and onto the path. The sun was just rising and he welcomed it as a Brother, thanking it for the light and life it would bring and congratulating Sister Moon on the night just passed. He walked with thankfulness for the day ahead of him.

As the path weaved uphill he felt the cords holding his shoe to his feet begin to weaken. Whilst many would have taken this as a sign they needed new shoes, Francis took them off genuinely excited by the possibility of walking with his bare feet touching Mother Earth. This was connection with God to Francis and reminded him that it had been a while since he had spent time in communing to the ground, taking in all that creation was and it's very heartbeat. (It's recorded Francis would often strip naked and lie down on the ground to be in as close proximity as he could to the created world.)

As he walked he heard the sound of birdsong. Francis liked to exhort the birds and other animals to praise God. This had been since he had noticed a flock of birds near Cannara looking attentively at him one day. Feeling compelled to speak to them he then noticed their apparent concentration and their song seemed to interact with him. All these created creatures were to him the fellow inhabitants of the earth and brothers and sisters to be cared for. Francis stopped as the birds flew over wishing them God's peace as they journeyed south.

Francis continued on, choosing to follow a babbling brook. He thanked God for the water and imagined all those who would be blessed by it's gentle flow. He began to sing as he walked along, seeming to intertwine a melody with the splashing of the water beside him.

Minutes became hours as he continued his journey. After miles had passed he felt a gentle ache in his body for the distance covered but thanked God for the staff that now supported him so ably. As he walked he met travellers on the way. He spent time saying hello to each he met and if welcome to share the gospel and to ask how he might serve them. Sometimes they would offer him bread or water which he would willingly accept. His greeting was always "Peace be with" and although this was not always received warmly, most were happy to smile and engage in some conversation. He liked to pray a blessing for strangers that he met and when they said yes it would warm his heart for the next part of his journey.

To many, Francis may have looked like a monk on the road but maybe to some a traveling troubadour, such was his joyful smile and willingness to sing and laugh as he went. GK

Chesterton called the Franciscans 'Jongleurs de deui' or troubadours of God. We know Francis was very influenced by the French troubadours or travelling performers who came through his town whilst he was a boy. He watched as they performed handstands as they came by and Chesterton muses whether Francis might perform a handstand as part of his worship.[16]

That day, Francis walked with a smile on his face and a song on his heart. As the light began to fade and his journey reached an end Francis found a fallen tree by the side of the road. Francis went over to the stump that remained in the ground and prayed for it's restoring, then he thanked God for the wood it provided and the seat that it gave him to rest his weary feet. He settled down, grateful for all God had given him that day.

---

[16] GK Chesterton 'St Francis of Assisi' Hodder & Stoughton 1946 (25th edition) pg 80

Day 25

Thought

In his biography of St. Francis, Adrian House declared "I propose Francis as a patron Saint for ecologists."[17] The World Wildlife Fund, chose to hold a conference of world's religious leaders in Assisi 1986, directly linking this cause to the work of Francis. Franciscan spirituality is expressed in brotherhood with creation.

Activity

Take a day where you ponder all of the natural world that is around you. Take time to notice animals, plants, trees, the sky. Write a poem or draw an image at the end of the day to reflect on what you've seen.

Prayer

Creator God, thank you for the world that you've made, that you give us the privilege to live in. Amen

---

[17] House 'Francis' pg. 10

Day 26

Thought

In The Canticle of the Creatures Chesterton observes that Francis "wanted to see each tree as a separate and almost sacred thing, being a child of God and therefore a brother or sister of man."[18]

Activity

Go to a busy place like a railway station or shopping centre. Consider how we share the world and the space we live in. What difference would it make to take this same view of the natural world. Take some time in silence.

Prayer

Create a simple chant and reflect on the natural world around you.

e.g.

Thank you for the sacred flowers that you made.
Thank you for the sacred river which revives us.

---

[18] Chesterton 'Francis' pg. 24

Day 27

Thought

Francis also viewed creation practically: exhorting cornfields and vineyards to serve God willingly by producing a crop.

Activity

Most church's calendars have harvest celebrations to celebrate and thank God for the provision of the land. This dates from times when this was very important to a person's survival. Organise a special meal and invite friends to celebrate the local produce of your area.

Prayer

Lord of the harvest thank you for food to eat and drink to drink. Thank you for what we have. Help us to act and to care for those who don't have enough. Amen

Day 28

Thought

Francis saw creation as something to live in harmony with. The story of him calming a wolf expressed the idea that both might live in harmony and although it sounds strange speaks of relationship. His language of Sun and Moon as Brother and Sister show a dependence and mutuality of living in this created earth.

Activity

Find an old set of scales and find different ways to balance them. Think about the idea of harmony and balance.

Prayer

God would you take my lack of balance and grant me equal weights. Would you take my broken view of the world I live in and make it straight.
Amen

Day 29

Thought

Francis' message was that we are living members of creation community. When we consider climate change could we stop tackling it as a project to be tackled or an obstacle to be overcome but instead a process of "fraternity" with the earth.

Activity

One of Francis' famous practices was to come into contact with the earth in his prayers - to lie on the ground so that he could embrace and celebrate this fraternity with the created world. Work out your own expression of this, maybe getting hands dirty in the garden, going walking or having a stone in your pocket throughout your day.

Prayer

Have a period of silence and reflection about climate change and global warming. Have some internet articles available about the issues. End your prayers with 'Have mercy Lord'.

Day 30

Thought

Francis was a wanderer but he did not wander in a void. He chose to take time and to appreciate all that was around him. He was able to notice the birds because he wasn't ignoring them and because they weren't superfluous to his greater aim of reaching journeys end. He could stop at a roadside and consider a lily.

Activity

At some point in your day pick a flower and press it in the pages of a book. Then when you have some time have a look at it. Reflect on Jesus' metaphor that we consider the lilies and how God provides.

Prayer

God thank you for the beauty of the lilies and for the provision you give to the smallest creatures in our world. Help us to trust you and to treat the earth's resources as a precious gift. Amen

Day 31

Thought

Francis' awareness of nature which enables him to take things at a different pace. Our focused living and overwhelming life pressures are not values we have picked up from the created world.

Activity

Place your hand on your heart and listen to your heartbeat for a while. Then concentrate on your breathing for a little while. Consider life rhythms which set a pace for our bodies. Which rhythms affect the way you live?

Prayer

God of creation who set in place simple rhythms for the world we live in, allow us to live in the unforced rhythms of grace in our own lives.

(Language adapted from the Message bible)

Day 32

Thought

One of the great Franciscan liturgies is the Canticle of the Creatures. In it Francis gives God glory for sun, moon, stars and for the blessing of the earth itself. All this perception of creation and our harmony with it led Francis to have a beautiful view of the glory of God and to practice it.

Activity

Go online and search for the text of the Canticle of the Creatures or find it in a Franciscan prayer book. Read it and write your own additional verses to give thanks for the things you love about the earth.

Prayer

Most High, all-powerful, good Lord,
all praise is yours, all glory, all honour,
and all blessing.
(From the Canticle of the Creatures)

MEETING WITH OURSELVES

"Rage belongs before God"
Bernd Janowski, theologian and writer

STORY: NAKED

This story takes us back to where we began, to the early part of Francis story.

As the last flickers of light were departing the day, the silhouette of a woman was visible walking from the door of her Assisi home to a set of outhouses nearby. She gently stepped down a small flight of steps to what appeared to be a hidden cellar. Moments later she could be seen ushering a very small and hunched man up the stairs. She hugged him and the immediately he headed off, walking quickly and purposefully. The woman stood and watched until he could be seen no more. Her head bowed and she stepped inside. Francis' mother had just released him from a captivity that had lasted a month and that had been instigated by his own father.

The story of this time locked up in a cellar and the story that was to follow have their roots in the wealth and influence of Francis' father Pietro. He was one of the leading cloth merchants in Assisi and as his business had grown combined with flourishing trade routes from Italy across Europe, Pietro's wealth deepened and expanded. He was a rich man and Francis was born into a rich family. For a while Francis had worked with his father until his short military career.

It could be said that Francis did not have a great relationship with money for the early part of his life. It's already been mentioned that biographers like Thomas Celano and Bonaventure were happy to mention his wild living in his youth. No mention was made of how Francis' parents felt about this but you can imagine Pietro urging the young Francis to uphold the family name and to prepare to take over the business one day.

But then Francis walked on his road of conversion and as he did so, money reared it's head again. As Francis began to understand the Jesus who loved those on the margins, he took to giving away large sums of money or food to the poor. This was Pietro's money and Francis had decided not to tell him. More than a year passed. His mother would sometimes assist him as he gathered food to give to the poor but his Dad never knew, that is until word began to get out.

First to hear about Francis and this generosity was Bishop Guido, the local bishop who was to become Francis' mentor. He must have been impressed with Francis, but concerned and aware that the wealth being given away was clearly not his own.

Then as Francis began to work at the church in San Damiano the local priest there was next to learn of this reckless generosity. He refused Francis' offer of large donations and in the end the young man took to rebuilding the church with his own hands. Now this new ministry for Francis was more out in the open and soon Pietro heard about it.

Returning from a business trip and hearing that Francis had been wasting his wealth, Pietro investigated fully and found out what Francis had been doing. He stormed down to the church where Francis was now living and shouted loudly outside the door, demanding the money back. Francis hid and did not answer. Such was the noise and the fuss Pietro made as he headed up that soon everyone knew of what had happened. All of Assisi's wealthy and important held Francis in contempt. For weeks Francis hid in his small hut but eventually he knew he needed to face his father. Stories suggest that as Francis walked into Assisi he was jeered at by local people and even pelted with rotten fruit. Pietro heard that Francis was coming, went to meet him and dragged him home, locking him in his cellar for several weeks. His mother Pica had compassion on Francis and would get food, water and care to him when she could. Then when Pietro left for another business journey, Pica slipped out of the house and released Francis. He fled back up to his hut near the church he was rebuilding but knew the matter had come to a head. He would have to face his father on his return. He began to pray for strength and guidance.

A few days later Francis walked up to Bishop Guido's house in Assisi. In his hands he held a bag of coins, all the money he had. The Bishop, in his desire to be kind to Francis (but also aware of the problems of Pietro's wealth being given away) had gathered them both in the hope he could broker a solution. As Francis walked in his father sat opposite in a chair, surrounded by a group of witnesses that Pietro had asked to attend to support his case. Their eyes met and both held a gaze of determination, but in very different ways.

Bishop Guido asked Pietro to lay out his accusations. Francis listened silently. The Bishop compassionately turned to Francis and asked him to resolve the problem. "Trust in the Lord, my son" he told him "for he will provide you with all that is needed for repairing the church."[19]

Immediately Francis stepped forward and agreed he would return his Father's money. Then without speaking he left the room. Everyone left with Bishop Guido looked surprised. First they had not expected such capitulation but now they were wondering where he had gone and what was going on. For several minutes there was complete confusion. Then the noise was broken by the

---

[19] Adrian House 'Francis' pg. 69

sound of footsteps and Francis returned. To everyone's horror he was completely naked.

"When he was in front of the bishop he neither delayed nor hesitated, but immediately took off and threw down all his clothes and returned them to his father. He did not even keep his trousers on, and he was completely stripped bare before everyone."[20]

Francis walked forward and placed his neatly folded clothes with the money bag on top right in the middle of Bishop Guido's elegant desk that stood in front of him.

Francis spoke and looked earnestly at everyone. "Please listen, everyone. Because I want to serve God from now on I am giving back to my father the money about which he is so distressed and also my clothes."[21]

---

[20] Thomas of Celano, "Life of St Francis First Book" from "Francis of Assisi: the Saint - Early Documents" New York: New York City Press 1999 pg. 189

[21] House 'Francis' pg. 69

In disgust Pietro picked up the clothes and money and left, leaving his son naked. The others present didn't know which way to look, amazed at what Francis had done and yet appalled that a father could leave his son in such a state. Bishop Guido though was already moving round his desk and towards Francis. Moved by such courage and devotion to God, Guido opened his arms and embraced him and as he did so he covered him with his cloak. Guido gave him a simple tunic to wear which he tied with a rope.

Francis left emboldened, released from the burden of his father's money but also filled with hope and expectation at what lay in front of him. Everyone there, including Francis, knew that something extraordinary had just taken place.

Day 33

Thought

In the early days of Francis' story it seemed he had to come to terms with a few demons. In his teenage years and in his twenties he had enjoyed wealth and all it's trappings. When his heart was turned towards faith he seemed to still live this out with money but now that option was gone. Sometimes we need a cultural reorientation as well as a spiritual one. What are the things that cloud our judgement today?

Activity

If you wear glasses take them off for a moment. Or if you don't put on some sunglasses or something that distorts your vision for a moment. What things in your life affect the way you think?

Prayer

In Romans 12:1 Paul says "Do not conform to the pattern of this world, but be transformed by the renewing of your mind." Reflect on this verse and turn it into prayer.

Day 34

Thought

The experience of Francis with his father forced him to confront a few things. As he sat in his simple hut whilst Pietro was away on business he knew he would have to confront him again. Several options must have existed for him. Was this faith thing really worth it? What was holding him back? He had to look into himself and be honest.

Activity

Its been said that the hardest step is always the next. As you walk today be mindful of your steps. What new or difficult things do you need to walk into? Be aware of the cost and what these steps might mean.

Prayer

Shakespeare once asked "boldness be my friend". Would the boldness of the Holy Spirit fill us today. Amen

Day 35

Thought

For Francis to make this break with the wealth and influence of his previous life he had to begin with small steps. Francis had been skulking in a small hut just by the church in San Damiano. He had been hiding from the world and the people who were against him. On the morning of the meeting with Bishop Guido and his father he had to begin with him leaving his hut, leaving his safe place. Imagine his first steps that day.

Activity

Remember your mindful walking yesterday. Draw a picture of a footprint and in it write an honest prayer of something you need to face up to or confront in your own life.

Prayer

Receive this honest prayer Lord and through it enable me to take my next faithful step. Amen

Day 36

Thought

Francis first handed over the coins to his father. He knew there was an element of theatre in this plan but there was also plenty of fear. Francis knew he needed to break all the ties that would stop him as he began the journey of new living. What might we need to hand over?

Activity

Pick up whatever spare change you have on you and place it in front of you. Consider honestly what hold money has on you. Consider a moment of generosity or something you can do to break the ties.

Prayer

Lord Jesus Christ you sustain us more than food, you supply us more than work and you support us more than money. Help us to trust you. Amen

Day 37

Thought

Francis had never fitted in and now as he took off his shirt and stood next door completely naked. Folding his clothes he knew that his moment of accepting this had arrived. Not fitting in was a gift and he was about to embrace it in vulnerability but also in determination.

Activity

Find two things that don't fit together - a square peg in a round hole maybe. Consider where you struggle to fit in. Is there anything God wants to say or that you want to say to God?

Prayer

Jesus, we remember in your life on earth that many thought you didn't fit in. Eventually this led to your death on the cross. Help us to embrace the gift of not fitting in and help us to live in a different and freeing way. Amen

Day 38

Thought

After all that stress, after weeks of prayer and heartache it was over. Francis was dressed in the brown tunic Bishop Guido had given him. He had no money but he knew he was better off. He had no safety net or fall back and his father would never speak to him again. He had to step out into the world.

Activity

Look out for the same brown colour of Francis' tunic today. When you see it in signs, cars or anything else (!) then think of Francis and this journey of reflection we've been on. Do this with a smile on your face if you can :-)

Prayer

Lord Jesus thank you for meeting Francis in that church in San Damiano. Thank you that this changed man helped to change our world. Help us to be change-makers too.

Day 39

Thought

If we, like Francis can deal with our demons and the things that seek to restrain us then we can imagine a new reality without fear. Then, just like him, anything is possible.

Activity

In the Harry Potter stories, students are asked to face a Boggle - a creature that takes the form of our darkest fears. The antidote is to imagine something stupid and then laugh at it. At that point it goes away. How might you laugh at your fears and overcome them?

Prayer

John wrote "perfect love drives out fear" (1 John 4:8). Fill us Lord with your perfect love so that we might find joy and hope instead of fear. Amen

Day 40

Thought

This is the final day of our reflections. What might one thing be to hold onto in the life of Francis. Consider your reflections. Realise that at the centre of all that Francis lived for was an absolute conviction in the love and life of Jesus. He looked to be like Him.

Activity

Write a spider diagram or brainstorm with all your thoughts and reflections about the life of Francis. Offer them to Jesus, his inspiration, as a prayer for your own life.

Prayer

Lord Jesus, who filled your servant Francis with your Spirit and through his and his brothers and sisters changed the world, fill us with that same Spirit and help us to love the poor, to love the world around us and to love You. In Jesus Name. Amen

Appendix:

Discovering more about Francis and Franciscans

This book has been created thanks in part to the influence of Franciscan monks and nuns I have met and Franciscan convents and friaries I have visited. In their honour I'd like to suggest five simple steps that you could take if you feel you'd like to know more about the little man from Assisi and the more than one million followers he has today.

Read a biography. There are many fantastic biographies of Francis. The one's which have most aided me in this project are 'Francis of Assisi' by Leonardo Boff (taking a liberation theology approach), 'Francis of Assisi' by Adrian House (an excellent chronological biography) and then 'St. Francis of Assisi' by GK Chesterton (a poetic and rather magical story of Francis from Chesterton's perspective). These are great books to get your teeth into. You may also want to find the early biographers by Thomas Celano and Bonaventure which are great first hand accounts but are much harder reads given the time they were written.

Visit a Friary or Convent. Many friars or convents are available to visit and to take retreats in. I'd recommend if you do this to join in with their collective worship and if possible to book an appointment with one of it's members. I loved my visits to Cold Ash in Newbury, to Hilfield in Dorchester and to the sisters at the Convent of the Incarnation in Oxford who were especially kind to me. Many places now have great websites and some offer specific guided visits/stays for those anxious to find out more. Use google to find places near you or consult http:// www.osffranciscans.com/

Find a spiritual director as ask them to help you explore Franciscan practices. This can be a great thing to do. A lot of dioceses/regions have directories of spiritual mentors/guides which you can access and many are Franciscan. Having someone of experience to accompany you can be incredible helpful and give you an understanding of the heart and reasoning behind some of the stories you hear.

Follow a Franciscan Prayer rhythm. I have become incredibly grateful to have a Franciscan prayer book and many are available. There are also smart phone apps and online prayer resources which can help you engage with Franciscan spirituality and practice.

The Third Order. I know an increasing number of friends who are considering the Franciscan Third Order, where you continue to live in the world but connect to a vow and a regular community. If this is something you're thinking about, make an appointment at your nearest OSF friary or convent and chat it through. There is a great process and helpful resources available to you. Don't do this lightly though as this is a serious step and there will be a long process of thought and preparation.

BIBLIOGRAPHY

Leonardo Boff 'Francis' New York: Orbis Books 2006

Adrian House 'Francis of Assisi' London: Pimlico 2001

Graham Cray and others "New Monasticism as a Fresh Expression of Church" Canterbury Press 2010

John V Kruse 'Lent and Easter Wisdom from St Francis and St Clare of Assisi' Missouri: Ligouri 2008

Shaine Claibourne 'The Irresistible Revolution' Michigan: Zondervan

Steven Bevans/Roger Schroeder "Constants in Context: A Theology of Mission for Today" New York: Orbis 2004

GK Chesterton 'St Francis of Assisi' Hodder & Stoughton 1946 (25th edition)

Thomas of Celano, "Life of St Francis First Book" from "Francis of Assisi: the Saint - Early Documents" New York: New York City Press 1999